I0435920

The New World Order Interview

By "The Scribe"

www.TheScribeBooks.com

For all those working for the progress of humanity.

Foreword

This is not a conventional book about the New World Order. Most books on the topic look at one or more particular subjects in detail to try proving the existence of a universal conspiracy to control humanity. A conspiracy known as the New World Order.

This book, however, is an interview with someone claiming to be a member of the families involved with running the New World Order. While it touches on what the theories are about, and briefly covers topics like the Freemasons and the central banks, it is much more a book of philosophy. A book about their purpose for a New World Order and how they justify their position of effectively ruling the world. As a book of philosophy, the book spends much of its time on the topics of Satan, Lucifer, and Christ, and even discusses some elements of the Bible and the prophets themselves.

So let this be fair warning that this interview looks at the New World Order from a totally different point of view, and steeps it all in a philosophy that's no doubt unexpected and perhaps unwanted by conspiracy theorists. But it is, after all, an interview. And it is, after all, what it is.

Finally, there may be those who want to know if this interview is real or imagined, and there may be those who are curious about the author. From my perspective as the author, though, the ideas here are the most important. Whether or not the interview happened, and whether or not the person interviewed was actually who he claimed to be, and who I am as a writer, are moot points. The goal here is simply to stimulate thought and perhaps discussion. Perhaps some will find the philosophies worth considering and acting on.

I hope that's enough to prepare you for something much different than the title might typically suggest, and to open your mind for playing with ideas.

—The Author
aka The Scribe.

Chapter 1

I sat in my study one evening surrounded with books and paper piles and empty cups of drinks long disappeared when I received the most surprising call of my life. Thinking it was a potential writing client, I turned on my phone and took the call.

"Is this S— M—?" asked an older man's voice.

"Yes, this is S—. How can I help?"

"I understand that you're playing a role in helping to establish the New World Order, and I've been instructed to sit and speak with you for a while about ... many things," he said. "To answer your questions and help in your work."

I laughed from sheer shock of the suggestion. "New World Order" is a term used in conspiracy theories referring to a movement by some dark groups to take control of the entire world. It was definitely *not* something I was helping to establish. These groups were supposed to have infiltrated governments and corporations everywhere in order to move them more or less as a team toward certain goals that would increasingly control and possibly kill off large numbers of the human population.

According to the theories, the New World Order controlled the mass media, the economy via central banks like the Federal Reserve, and the laws not only as politicians but also as those pulling political strings. They were everywhere, like a bad cancer in the body of humanity. They were believed by most to run the Freemasons (though most Freemasons would never know or believe it) and possibly to be Satanists. And there were a lot of separate but related theories about methods of dumbing down the population, eliminating its moral compass, preparing for total communication and transportation control, and even embedding the population with computer chips for tracking people and for running a fully digital economy. In fact, since it was easiest to take control of an unarmed population, some of these theories further believed the New World Order was behind the effort to ban guns in the USA.

I, on the other hand, had already written a novel about a couple of guys who lived in a world of political and corporate corruption at a time when Earth's government had gone global. While it touched on both sides of many topics, like political leadership and taxes and conspiracies, the theme was pretty clearly *not* in favor of controlling people, but about having them come together for their common purpose.

So to think that I was helping to establish the New World Order was really a hoot, and the only thing I could fathom was that someone was playing a prank on me. "Who is this?" I asked. "Who asked you to call?"

"You may know me as N.G.," said the caller. "I can explain more about who had me call when we get together."

"But I know this is a joke," I said. "Obviously I'm not trying to help set up the New World Order. I think you're trying to reach the Rothschildses." I chuckled. The Rothschildses were one of the families believed to be at the core of the New World Order movement.

"No," he said, ignoring my attempt at humor. "I was explicitly told to contact you. Aren't you working toward a one world government? And a single currency? And probably a digital currency? I was told you believed in all these things."

"Now wait a second," I said. "First, I don't know what you mean by working toward these things. I'm not in much of an influential position to make things like that happen. I write what I write. I promote certain ideas. But on a very small scale to those who happen to stumble across my writing."

"Yes," said he, "but these things always start on a small scale. We can easily get your writing in front of the whole world if we want to. I just need to make sure you have the information you need to get it right."

His comment surprised me, but it didn't stop me. "That's not even the main point," I said. "Whether I have one person or a million reading my work, I'm not necessarily promoting a one world government or single currency. I just think that they're inevitable. And despite many people's fears about both, I think they would actually fix a lot of our current problems while obviously creating some new problems of their own."

"Yes," said the man, sounding like he agreed.

"As for digital currency, I'm not sure that's the solution. I just believe we have to do *something* to wrestle control of our financial system out of the hands of a few central bankers and into the collective hands so that we have better control of our own destiny. That might end up good or bad, but it's better than having some hidden group manipulating interest rates and people's abilities to earn a living wage."

"That's a curious thought," said the man. "I can see how you would think that would be better. But the moment that the corrupt masses turned that into a fiasco and plummeted the world into the worst possible depression, you might feel differently. In any case, I can see that I'm speaking with the right person. So when would you like to meet?"

"Ha!" I laughed accidentally. I quickly recovered myself. "I'm sorry, but I'm not sure I agreed to meet. Obviously I'm saying that I'm not part of the New World Order."

"Oh, that's not at all obvious to me. What's clear to me is that you misunderstand the New World Order and your role in helping it to come about."

"I ... well ...." I stopped speaking. What was I supposed to say to that? "Well what is *your* role in it? How do *you* have any information? And again, who told you to call?"

"If I answer these questions, will you agree to meet?" he asked.

I hesitated. I didn't know who this was and, to me, this was a pretty dangerous topic. Get involved with the wrong people here and you could disappear, far as I was concerned. It didn't take much of a conspiracy theory to be concerned about that. I was pretty sure that political dissidents disappeared every day and we probably didn't hear about most of them.

"Seems a little safer if we meet near my home," I said.

"Of course," he agreed. "I understand there is a beautiful hotel in your town. I can take a suite for us to meet in. Would that be satisfactory?"

This concerned me. He obviously knew where I lived, which meant he had already researched me, and I didn't know if that put my family at risk. He could hear my hesitation. "I'm afraid there's not much I can say to make you trust me, but I assure you that you're under no obligation or threat. I am told that you earnestly want to make a difference in the world, and we're opening the doors for you to do so."

This piqued my interest just enough to nod to myself. "Ok," I said. "Answer my questions well enough and we'll meet at the hotel."

"Very good," he said. "As I said, you may know me as N.G. I speak on behalf of one of the seven families that *you* would call leaders of the New World Order. There are also seven leading families that, in your mind, would oppose the New World Order. Your work has come to their attention, and they have asked that I sit down with you to reveal what you need."

My eyes narrowed. First, it was hard to believe that they had noticed my work, given that I didn't think many people had read my books or online content. But even then: "If my work came to their attention, why would they ask *you* to speak with me?"

"Because," said N.G., "they want to make sure you have a balanced understanding so you can start to set the record straight and help people understand the purpose of the New World Order."

So it existed then. The New World Order. This thing that many people thought was a fearful fancy by delusional militia members. At least it existed according to this person. And now things were just too interesting to ignore. "When do we meet?" I asked.

Chapter 2

Two weekends later, N.G. came into town and booked the largest suite at the nearby hotel. As I reached his floor of the hotel, I passed through a sitting area in the hallway where a barrel-chested man stood from the couch. "Mr. M—," he said, "if you don't mind, I just need to do a quick check before I walk you to his room." A hired goon! I couldn't believe I actually had a hired goon approaching me! But I shrugged and let him do a quick metal sweep with a handheld device. He then walked me down the hall and swiped a keycard to let me into a room.

N.G. was waiting inside and welcomed me, dismissing the goon back to his post. N.G. appeared to be at least in his seventies and on the verge of frail, but he shook my hand firmly as I entered the room. His blue eyes seemed sharp, but he also looked somehow tired, as if life had gone on for plenty long.

Still, he couldn't have been more gracious. After a handshake, he gestured toward the dining room table, which held a gorgeous spread of breads, cheeses, fruits, and desserts alongside carafes of coffee, a selection of teas, and bottles of wine. At a hotel like this, I knew a spread like that didn't come cheap. Two of the terrace doors were open slightly to let in a breeze and the vigor of fresh air from the warm day.

I grabbed a coffee and a plate piled with fruit, then joined him at a coffee table beside an unlit fireplace. N.G. was seated on the couch on one side and I found myself a chair opposite him, setting my food on the coffee table before settling in. As I did so, N.G. looked kindly at me as he seemed to think about how to begin.

"So the New World Order," he said. "You're not too fond of the idea?"

I'd read a lot about the New World Order over the years, partly because it was related to legitimate political concerns and partly because it was just interesting reading, even when (or especially when?) it started to sound entirely like fiction. The topic was involved in questions about what the media covered, why so many political decisions seemed to go against the good of the people, how our financial system was run, and how foreign policies were decided on, including our engagement in wars — declared or otherwise.

When you read about people's ideas on the New World Order, you run into all sorts of fears and wild theories in addition to ideas that make sense if you let your mind ask questions. Mainstream thought has tried lumping all of these into a pile called conspiracy theories. By putting them all in one basket like this, authorities can more effectively make all the theories look like the rantings of crazy people, making them easy to criticize and sweep under the rug.

But it doesn't take much of a political wizard to look at history and know that corruption has always been part of politics, and that there are plenty of conspiracies between those who want power for themselves. You don't have to believe in every conspiracy theory, or even believe that there is a single global conspiracy to form a New World Order, to believe that there are a lot of legitimate concerns being voiced in these discussions. But if there was, in fact, a goal to develop a world government that would further control the population, that was something I was against. "I have to say," I told the gentleman, "that I'm not a fan."

"So I've spent some time thinking about where to start explaining, and I realized that we need to get past this term New World Order so you understand what we're really talking about. As far as you know, where does that term come from?"

"Seems like the first President Bush started using the term when he was in office. Others have used it since. And the United States seal uses a similar term in Latin referring to a new order of the ages."

"Well sure it does," said N.G. "It's a term coined by Virgil before Christ, and wouldn't you say that the United States was first formed with a goal of breaking away from the old world in Europe and establishing a new order?"

I shrugged. "Sure."

"See, there's nothing wrong with a new order. At the time, the United States was seeking to be a new national order. A new way of doing things, thus a new order of the ages, or of its time period. But today, things have so greatly sped forward, and we operate on a global basis now. I think there's no denying that. So if we take away any stigma from that term — if you can pretend you'd never heard that term before — then tell me, would you prefer to be part of the old world order, the way things have always been, or would you prefer to see change. Progress. A new world order?"

I thought I should gulp, because he had me. But I kind of laughed, because he had me. "Ok," I chuckled, "I get that. The term itself has a positive meaning if it means progress for the people. But that's just playing with words. When we use that term today, we're talking about an effort by certain groups to control all the people under one government. So whether or not it's a reality, whether or not there are groups trying to do this, it's not a positive term the way it's used."

"No?" he asked, raising his eyebrows in surprise. "Is that because you don't want the people to be controlled, or because you're against a world government?"

"It's more about the control of the people, taking away their freedom to express the best that's in them. If we had one world government that allowed people more freedom than they have today, I'd probably be for it. Because maybe that would limit some of the constant warring, which is part of what enslaves people anyway. But if I know anything about government, I'd bet that one world government would promise to eliminate war, but then would use its unified resources to increasingly watch people; to freely access the most precious gifts of the world for the benefit of the 1%; and to *still* have a standing military as a global police force to keep the people under thumb. Government has always sought control for the benefit of those in the government, so this just makes sense to me."

"Ok, fair enough," said N.G. "So it sounds to me like we're agreeing on a couple of points. A new order isn't a bad thing in and of itself. And global government could be a good thing or a bad thing, depending on how it functions and how it benefits the people. Is that a fair way to put it?"

I shrugged again. "I guess I can't argue with that. Although there's still the question of national sovereignty and identity that some people are worried about."

"Sure," said N.G. "Much the way the States were concerned about this when they agreed to be gathered under a federal government. Obviously today the States still have their own identities. And we can sit here and argue about whether the Federal government has overstepped its bounds on making laws, but the concept is that the States retain control over intrastate matters and the Federal government controls interstate matters. Maybe that needs to be better executed. But if a world government were formed on the same concept, wouldn't that be a natural next step in human governance?"

"I would think so. It's why I feel it's inevitable. But obviously people see the Federal government passing laws that we think should be decided by the States, and we're concerned the same thing would happen on a global scale. In fact, you already see it happening with a lot of international treaties trumping national law."

"Yes, I see the concern," said N.G. "But again, conceptually, you can see that as the natural evolution of government. And if it were executed well, it would be similar to the ideals set forth in the U.S."

"Seems that way," I admitted.

"Good. And then of course, digital or not, this would lead to a global currency, much the way the U.S. Federal currency eliminated previous bank currencies and foreign currencies from use in the States. Right?" I nodded. It only made sense if government went global. "So again, this could be bad news if the government wasn't looking out for the good of the people. Or it could be good news in your eyes if the government stopped tracking and controlling people the way it does today, right? In other words, a single currency isn't the problem, but how the government is run?"

I couldn't see anything wrong with this argument, so I nodded. After all, I wasn't sure how much longer the U.S. dollar would be worth anything given the way we allowed runaway printing of our currency and approached $20 trillion dollars of debt, not to mention future obligations. It might be inevitable that it would lose its status as the world currency, and I wasn't sure I wanted one other country to have the kind of currency power we'd had up to this point. Better that we be on a level playing field with others.

"So just to really confirm, the concept of a new world order isn't the problem. The concept of one world government or one world currency isn't the issue. The real issue, in your mind, is control of the people. You don't want them giving up their rights, being tracked, being forced into certain decisions, and so on. You want people to be free." I nodded. More than anything, I wanted people to be able to live up to their potentials, and government seemed to be one of the primary hurdles to this.

"Great," said N.G. "Then I want to tell you that we're really very much on the same page, though our emphasis is a little different than yours. Unfortunately, like a lot of people, you feel that this difference in emphasis makes us the bad guys. But you know, it's very two-dimensional to see just good guys and bad guys, like everything is black and white. You probably know that as a writer. You have the guy that everyone's rooting for, and the guy everyone's against, but it's never a great story if the good guy has no flaws or the bad guy has no legitimate motivation besides being evil. Usually, the so-called bad guy believes he's doing the right thing. In this matter of the New World Order, I will gladly admit that our seven families have worked hard to control the human race, and also that we're convinced that our work has been good and necessary.

"That's why your work came to certain people's attention. You were looking at both sides of many issues, and it was felt that you could understand: our emphasis and yours are two sides of the same coin. And without our side playing a role, you'd have run into large-scale chaos and destruction long ago."

"How so?" I asked.

"Because one part of human nature is incredibly destructive, and by controlling the population, we have reined in that destruction to some degree. Enough to keep the race alive and developing. So while you think that we've been against human freedom, that's not entirely true. We've been against the freedom of its destructive force, which in turn *has* provided a kind of freedom to people. The freedom to continue living, and to develop a society, you see? To do this, we've thrown a broad blanket of control that people have never been happy about. Nevertheless, it has been to the population's benefit.

"Of course this is the basis of the ongoing debate of security versus freedom. Until people can all control their destructive side, they must be controlled for the sake of the whole. But as more people be-come capable of controlling that side of themselves, they increasingly want to be free — since they've earned that freedom — in order to express the best of what's in them. But if you remove control for one person, do you remove it for everyone? If not, how is that fair? And if you do remove it for everyone for the sake of those who have earned it, how does that keep people safe when there are still destructive people in the world? You see how complicated this is?"

I nodded. "I understand the concept," I said, "but there's no question that government has grossly overstepped its bounds and is serving spe-cial interests more than it's serving the people."

"In one sense, that's true, and we'll talk more about that. In another sense, there are still terrorist attacks. Still people hurting others. So arguably, we're still not controlling people enough. But setting that aside, let me ask: if you were able to magically figure out exactly how much government should control people, and if those controls weren't abused, wouldn't you see how *some* element of control is a good thing? A necessary thing?"

"If it controlled people to the extent that they should control themselves anyway, then I guess those who naturally controlled themselves wouldn't feel any additional restriction from government," I said. "And they could focus on making their own choices about health and raising their kids and supporting the public good through charities rather than through taxes and so on."

"And would you admit that, if you were dictator and could set all the boundaries of control exactly where they ought to be ... would you admit that it would be a very difficult job to do that perfectly?"

I laughed. "Yes, I sometimes think about that. As easy as it is to see how politics are abused by special interests, I also think about how tough it is to make perfect laws. To get the results you're hoping for. Too many factors to consider. Too many ways that people will respond to the law, some trying to comply with it and others trying to avoid it."

"So on the one hand," said N.G., "we do have people trying to control the population as a necessary measure. And I'll talk later about the abuse of this process. But understand that this control is actually for a kind of freedom, and was actually the ideal for a long time.

"Still, there is admittedly a higher ideal that people like you want to see," said N.G. "The ideal where humans no longer have to be controlled by outside forces. Where everyone can live freely and express the best of what's in them. I admit that this would lead to an incredible human experience, full of health and abundance and innovations and personal fulfillment. So it's a beautiful thing to promote, but it's also naive when you ignore the chaos of removing control, which would allow more people to hurt others. You cannot have your ideal of freedom without first having the ideal of control. It's a paradox, I know, but so is most of life. So when I hear people demonizing government control in their discussion of freedom, I know that they don't understand how these two ideals work together. After all, it's easy to promote freedom when you've never been a serious victim of the worst aspects of humanity. But when you've been injured by others, then you realize that control *does* promote freedom, though it's a different level of freedom, you see?"

I nodded. I understood the challenge of this debate on security and freedom. And while I definitely wanted to see change in everything from government to business to education and more, while I wanted to see us better promote the potential of humanity, I couldn't argue with the points he made. There was a kind of freedom gained by protection from the worst elements.

"I get all that," I said. "I even understand the challenge of figuring out how much control is the right amount. But government doesn't even come close when it comes to protecting people from its own abuses as a government; or from the banks or lawyers or corporations. Seems to me that they're tracking and controlling people, but not doing anything like protecting us."

"Oh," said N.G., "you can hardly imagine all the protections in place. But you're absolutely right about the abuses, as I said before. And I'll explain that as we go along. But for now, you see that there are two forces in place. One seeking to control humanity, which actually promotes a certain kind of freedom; and another seeking to bring humanity up to the next level of freedom ... the kind of freedom more and more people are demanding today. And this issue of control versus a higher freedom is the matter that fourteen families have largely guided on this planet for thousands of years."

Chapter 3

"So these are the families you mentioned before. Seven families that are promoting the New World Order and seven that are against it. And you're speaking on behalf of one of the families promoting this Order."

N.G. smiled. Then he leaned back in his chair, folded his hands in front of his face with his index fingers pointed upwards and tapped those fingers gently against that smile. He was observing me and thinking. "Not quite," he told me. "When I explained that before, I said that's the way *you* would see it. That we were for the New World Order and the other families were against it. But here's the revelation: we're all working toward a New World Order, and that includes your own work whether you know it or not. All the families want to see a single world government and a single currency. The difference is in control of the people. Our seven families want to continue tightly controlling the population for the reasons I've explained. The other seven families want to help them reach their next level of potential. Or, as you might put it, to set them free.

"Either way, a one-world government allows the objectives to move forward much more easily. One government with access to the entire population can dominate them all without going outside its jurisdiction; or on the other hand can actively promote freedom without leaving its jurisdiction. Take some of your more dangerous, terrorist groups today — imagine if the one government needed no permission to whip those groups into line without worry that another government would get in its way. You see?"

I nodded. "Yes, but what gives you the right to control other people? What makes you so important that you can manipulate laws and economies and media? I mean, your families are doing those things for control, right?"

"Certainly. It would be silly to deny that. The conspiracy theories are right in a lot of ways, but they're also missing a lot of important information, like why we're doing this and how it all works, and where it really gets out of our hands.

"To answer your questions, I don't think the families consider themselves more important than other humans in a spiritual sense, though we do consider ourselves in a special position of service to the human family. This doesn't make us better or worse, but admittedly fairly unique in what we do. Now when you want to talk about what gives us the right from a strictly worldly perspective, the physical reality is that we have the right because we have the power. In other words, if you only look at things from a worldly view, then power is the only thing that gives anyone rights, and so-called God-given rights are a laugh. So if we're just talking about power, then clearly we have the money and power to do what we're doing. End of story.

"But if you were to ask why we *believe* we have the authority — the moral authority — you'd get a very different answer. Because we don't just believe in a worldly view of things. I'm not saying you need to agree with our view; I'm only saying that this is how we see things.

"In our eyes, we come from a spiritual lineage that extends back to humanity's earliest days. There were always two spiritual lines of people known as the prophets. One line destined to control humanity in the sense we've talked about; and one destined to promote its freedom. The prophets of control would allow humanity to survive; the prophets of freedom would help humanity to reach its potential. So you see, both lines of prophets were leaders given to humankind from the highest wisdom, even if humans — who hate to restrict themselves no matter how good it might be for them — think that these prophets are a curse. So you have thought our seven families — the families of control — to be evil. But as I explained before, we have allowed humanity to survive. Do you understand?"

His question, directed at me, brought my awareness back to myself, and I found that both my eyebrows were raised with interest and in disbelief. "Well yes, I understand why you think it's important to control people. But I'm not sure I buy into this idea of lineage. Which, by the way, sounds a lot like the stories of you running the Masons, who claim an ancient lineage."

"Well remember, you don't have to buy into my story of spiritual lineage; only to understand that this is our answer to your question, why we have the right to control. From our perspective, it is a God-given right; actually a God-given task. In fact, while I won't reveal the true name of the controlling lineage, many people are familiar with the name Melchizedek — the priesthood of Christ. That is the lineage of the other seven families.

"As for the Freemasons," continued N.G., "there is again truth and distortion in the theories. Early Masons based the teachings of their brotherhood on some of what they saw from the prophets, but they didn't have access to the private teachings of either family. So it does make sense to say that there are inner teachings not known to the vast majority of Masons, as some conspiracy theories suggest. Also that the 'inner circle,' so to speak, is indeed seeking to promote a New World Order, as I've explained this term. But this inner circle — the fourteen families, I mean — wouldn't consider itself at all in control of the Masonic order, or really part of it. The Masons have been around a long time, and do have some valuable teachings and charitable efforts. But the organized Masonic order really has nothing to do with running the world." N.G. smiled as if taking a little pleasure in putting that particular conspiracy theory to rest.

"So there is no Illuminati?" I asked. The Illuminati were supposed to be *the* inner circle of the Masons. As the name suggests, they were the self-described enlightened ones that really ran the show, and were sort of at the center of the entire New World Order scheme of things. This was a group feared by a lot of conspiracy theorists, and some of their writings definitely seemed to put themselves above the rest of humanity, as if they ought to control and shape the population.

"On the contrary," said N.G., "we're talking all

about the Illuminati here. Again, the theories have half the story right, but they don't understand the context. What does Illuminati mean?"

"Something like 'the enlightened,'" I said.

N.G. nodded. "And wouldn't you consider enlightenment a good thing?" he asked.

"Sure. Genuine enlightenment, yes. But this is something that someone *is* or *isn't*. If he's truly enlightened, it's not something he makes claims about, and this doesn't put him above the rest of humanity."

"Not in terms of eternal value as a soul," agreed N.G. "We're all equal in that regard. But enlightenment certainly refers to someone in a more advanced stage of service. What's more, the Illuminati simply refers to those who are enlightened, relatively speaking; it's not a structured organization, but a concept, much like calling someone a Christian doesn't place them into one particular church, but into a way of thinking.

"What's more, this isn't a group that's made claims to others about its own enlightenment. In fact, it's attempted to be quiet about itself for exactly the reason that one doesn't brag of one's enlightenment. This doesn't stop Illuminati from recognizing one another by word and deed, or inviting one another to gather in organizations, just as other people of like mind do. This tendency for being quiet also doesn't stop others from reading our materials or otherwise knowing something about us and claiming that we're a secret organization specifically *because* we're quiet about ourselves.

"Think of it like this: let's say that Christianity wasn't a religion, but that a lot of people believed in the teachings of Christ and attempted to live up to his ideals. Those largely living by his ideals might consider themselves Christians, even though there was no organized religion. And because those Christians would typically share many ideals and goals, they might even get together in groups apart from other people for simple camaraderie and even to promote their mutual ideals of brotherhood. They might not talk much about their Christianity publicly because others might scorn their most precious beliefs; so instead they might meet privately and then go out into the world and promote their Christian goals through their work rather than through open teachings. Within their own circles, they would certainly discuss their beliefs, and others could find out about those beliefs and call them a secretive organization. Would this make Christians bad people? In my mind, this is exactly what we mean by Illuminati. It's a reference to those with certain beliefs and goals and, in our minds, a certain level of spiritual development. Since the Illuminati are not all of one religion, however, we use this more universal term referring to enlightenment."

"But no devil worship or anything like that?" I asked. "A lot of people associate the Illuminati with Lucifer or Satan."

"Well those are two entirely different concepts, grossly misunderstood in the modern mind," said N.G. "In past writings, 'lucifer' was just a description or title — it meant 'shining one.' Old writings even used this term to refer to Christ and, except in the King James version of the Bible, 'Lucifer' is never used as a Biblical name. It's a relatively recent phenomenon that 'Lucifer' became a name for Satan, and this is entirely inaccurate.

"Yet this really brings us into the crux of our conversation. I've been talking with you about two forces that were necessary for humanity, to prevent chaos. I've said that both actually promoted freedom of a certain kind, although in modern terms, people tend to see one as control and the other as freedom. But if these two forces were needed to prevent chaos, then there is a third force — chaos itself. So we're not really talking about two forces, but three, and people would understand the world much more accurately if they thought about all three. People have an inaccurate sense of things, believing only in good and evil. But it's much more interesting than that. Care to be 'enlightened'?"

I laughed at the Illuminati reference and nodded. "Fair enough. Three forces, and two of them are promoted by families of prophets. Enlighten me."

Chapter 4

"Let's talk more broadly about the concept of God. I think that will make this easier," said N.G. I nodded again as I took a sip of coffee. "Would you agree that God is generally considered to be all powerful and present everywhere?"

"Sure," I said, setting my mug back on the coffee table.

"So we have this idea of Satan as the antithesis or opposite of God. But if God is all powerful and everywhere, doesn't that mean that Satan has no power and is nowhere?"

I laughed, and was glad I had already swallowed my drink. "Yes, if you take Satan as a literal opposite."

"So basically we understand that Satan can't literally be an opposite of God, because such a thing would be nothing." I nodded again, and thought it a little strange that I found myself in so much agreement with someone I was pretty sure was part of a conspiracy to control humanity. At least if what he said was true.

"This should make us question, then, what evil is," said N.G. "And the way our families see evil is anything that slows down or attempts to reverse the spiritual development of humanity. Anything that keeps people from moving toward God. Is that a fair definition?"

"It's pretty simple," I said. "But simple works for me as a concept."

"Well then, I can tell you that both lines of prophets indeed believe in evil, and although its true name on our planet is not Satan, we can use that name for the concept. It's basically come to be known as Satan in the Western culture. This is not an individual being of evil; it is much more subtle than that. Much more difficult. Do you remember the old quote, 'We have met the enemy, and he is us?'"

"Sure," I said, smiling. "From the old Pogo comics."

"Right. So I mentioned that we're not dealing with two forces of light and darkness, good and evil. We're dealing with three. None of them is inherently evil, because each has its purpose in creation. The first force is the body consciousness. It is all about survival of the individual at the cost of anything and everything else. It makes sure that a creature will feed itself, get shelter, and do the other things necessary for survival. You see — things at the bottom of Maslow's hierarchy of needs.

"This would be especially dangerous if the individual didn't see some survival value in forming a family unit and, in a larger sense, a clan. Because of this, cooperation is formed, and the individuals aren't all at each other's throats. But at its core, this is only for selfish reasons. This force only cares about the individual, and it is what we call the satanic force. It is an intelligence, yes, but it is an animal intelligence. Notice how Satan is often depicted as a goat. There are reasons why the goat was used, but this still refers us to the animal intelligence of Satan."

"In other words," I said, understanding his point, "there is a purpose for this force. It's not a force directly opposed to God, but since it's totally selfish, it takes us backwards these days when we're trying to become more of a human family. And if it takes us backwards, it's something we consider evil."

"Bingo!" said N.G. pointing at me. "And if Satan were the only force on Earth, humans would never be more than animals, living in small family or clan units with each individual primarily seeking benefits for him or herself. Sacrifices for others would be unknown outside of those for one's offspring, which is also part of the survival instinct. Because Satan only sacrifices others for his own good. Never the other way around, because that fails his singular goal of survival. That is his *only* goal, you see. And it's a valuable goal. But it's far behind the goals of humanity. It's only an animal goal. Since this force is in everyone, the basis of our physical existence, we are indeed our own enemy."

"So I'm guessing that brings up the other two forces," I said.

N.G. nodded and took a sip of tea before explaining that. "Yes. When God created humans, he — if I can use the masculine here — he created humans in his own image, as the Bible says. This means they were created as more than just animals; they were created with the ability to receive and act from light, or truth, in a way that animals cannot; and they were created with the ability to receive and act from love in a way that animals cannot.

"This is not to say that the light and love of God are not in animals, but that they were not designed to receive and act from these in the same way. Animals are primarily Satanic — and remember, that doesn't mean evil. It means they're survival oriented."

"What about pets and the affection they can show?" I demanded.

N.G. sighed. "I don't want to get too far off track with these details," he said. "But briefly, first remember that 'satanic' doesn't mean 'evil.' Second, remember that affection can come from survival instincts, or from the intellect, or from the heart. All of these can express what looks like affection, even in humans. I can't tell you how many family interactions among humans are based on survival rather than light or love. So yes, the seeds of light and love are in animals, and in my mind domesticated animals have sprouted these seeds and begun to express them more than your typical wild animal. This is an important point to humans having pets.

"But again, let's not get off track. Let's stick with this basic idea that these two forces of light and love — how they're received and used — separate humans from animals. Separate them from Satan, you see? Light and love. Two forces, and two lines of prophets established from the beginning, inspired by these forces. And between light and love, guess which is more powerful."

I was staring skeptically at him, but responded more or less automatically. "Love," I said.

N.G. smiled again and shook his head. "No. It's a trick question. Neither is more powerful. They need each other. Together, they are the expression of God because God is both. Love, however, couldn't be introduced to humans in the beginning. It is so incompatible with the satanic element that it would destroy anyone with too much Satan in them, so to speak. Satan's selfish survival nature had to be restricted in people before they could receive the full force of love. So the light of truth — the 'law' — had to be introduced, to take control of the population. And in modern terms, how have we personified light?"

I furrowed my brows. "The sun?" I asked doubtfully, knowing that was a symbol and not personification. "Or Christ?"

"No no," said N.G. "The prophets of Christ — the Melchizedeks — bring the love. That is the other family line. They've had to wait for humans to restrict Satan before they could rise in power. But we already talked about this personification of light. About the shining one."

Then I realized: "Lucifer."

"Yes," said N.G. "The Bringer of Light. A whole line of prophets was established to bring the light to humanity and, in modern terms, we would be known as followers of Lucifer, but only so far as Lucifer is a personification of the light. Of course many people have confused Lucifer with Satan, so we're considered pretty awful people, you see?"

"Well that, and the fact that you're controlling the population," I pointed out.

"But as I've explained, this was exactly our purpose. Our directive from God. Without love and light, humanity was satanic. Since love couldn't be introduced first to overcome Satan, light had to be introduced to overcome Satan. To control Satan. To control the animal nature of humanity. So our families were given first control. We were given the law, which was originally based only on the light of truth. And truth, if you didn't know it, can be brutally cold and harsh when it's not warmed with love. Nevertheless, it was necessary.

"And of course the truths that we've used to control humanity have also been distorted by the satanic element in a million ways, for Satan still has plenty of its own power on Earth. This is why human law looks so little like divine law, light, or truth. But we've done our job laying down the law — what to do and what not to do according to the divine inspiration that our families received. The Old Testament and other sacred texts are full of these laws of light. They are all about controlling the lower satanic element, you see? Don't kill, don't steal, don't lie — all things that Satan is happy to do, and that would destroy the race if not controlled.

"Of course to promote the law, we were given much power over humanity — the power to set up rulers and economies, for instance, and to change them as we saw fit. This is still our role, and it makes us look quite privileged to those who don't realize the responsibility we've been given. The average person resents us if they know about us; they think it unfair that we control so many resources; but we have done so to their benefit, as much as they won't want to admit it."

"Ok," I said to N.G. as I shifted in my chair, getting ready to argue just a bit. "So this explanation makes your families sound like good guys. And you've claimed that you consider yourselves equals with the rest of humanity, even if you serve in a unique way. But I've read some things that are supposed to be Illuminati writing, and they sound awfully elitist. And some folks are concerned that the New World Order is anti-Christian. What do you say about that?"

"Well I'm not sure specifically what writing you're talking about, but I admit that there is a lot of illuminated writing that speaks about the lowly nature of humanity before it has been refined. And since many humans have yet to refine the animal nature, then yes, our perspective could sound elitist. Because we believe those with light should naturally be in charge, controlling the unenlightened. After all, the unenlightened will destroy things, given that they are satanic in nature. If that sounds elitist to you, then we are elitists. We don't want humanity to be destroyed.

"On the topic of Christianity, you must remember that we are luciferic. That is our God-given purpose. This doesn't mean that we oppose the Christ influence. Ultimately, we believe that influence will reign, and we believe this to be the divine plan. Until that time, we will continue our work of controlling Satan. Since this is about control rather than the freedom promoted by the Melchizedeks, it might look anti-Christian. But if you want to understand the true anti-Christian influence, it is the satanic element that opposes Christ. That is because the animal is afraid of giving up the control it thinks it has on things. It sees this as a threat. So it fights against giving up control to the power of Christ.

The light, however, knows that it does not lose itself when Christ gains power. Instead, the light is fulfilled. There is, after all, light in the love of Christ. Our purpose is best fulfilled when Christ reigns. So no, we are not against Christ. Satan is. And Satan is the animal in every person. The enemy within.

"Remember that when Christ was here, he specifically said that he didn't come to destroy the law and the prophets, but to *fulfill* them. You see? He was specifically referring to our line of prophets and the law we had laid down. The prophets of light, and the law itself, would be fulfilled when the love of Christ reigned. But as the law was fulfilled, it also came to look different. Rather than an eye for an eye, Jesus taught people to love their enemies. This was not in opposition to the law, but lifted it to a far more refined form. Rather than transforming the enemy and oneself through punishment, one transforms everything through love. This is what Christ sought for humanity, and what he planted for the future.

"On this topic of who is Christian, though, I should point out something that will make a lot of people uncomfortable. Even angry," said N.G.

"What's that?" I asked, furrowing my brows. He'd already said plenty that could upset people and never prefaced it with a statement like this. I wondered what could warrant this kind of warning.

"Satan, as I've said, is in every human. It is the animal nature, and while it has its use in the animal kingdom, it is precisely what humans are supposed to overcome. This is hereditary sin or Original Sin. And of course any time someone acts from this nature, they are satanic. This isn't a judgment — as you can see, I'm just defining what it means to be satanic, and in that case, they are satanic.

"That's probably not much of a surprise to most people since many already believe in some kind of hereditary sin or at least in a battle between good and evil inside themselves," N.G. continued. "But here's the truth that most won't want to hear: when people lay down the law, when they judge others even according to the light of truth, this is usually luciferic. This is because most human hearts — while beginning to open to the love of Christ — are largely not yet functioning the way they're destined to. Christ is gradually being born in humanity, and this will totally transform the planet. But until that happens, then people are luciferic even when they're doing their best to be good. This is because they're doing good for intellectual reasons; doing good from the light. They're not doing it because of a throbbing passion of love for humanity, as they will when Christ is fully alive in their hearts. In other words, when they're at their best, people are the very thing that they fear — they are luciferic, just as our families are. They are like the people who have been controlling them with external force for so long."

"Except when they're at their best, they're only controlling *themselves*," I argued. "They're not controlling other people like your families do."

N.G. laughed. "I would disagree. When acting from the light, people continually make judgments about the world around them, and they try to control it in the way they think yields the most good. This means they're often trying to control others, whether in subtle or obvious ways. They're doing exactly what we've done, though we've done it as a group and on a large scale."

I frowned at this, but mainly because it made sense. "You're talking about religious radicals?" I asked. "People who take ideas from the Bible or other religious texts and persecute others?"

N.G. shrugged. "In one sense, yes. Maybe they're the most obvious. But I'm also talking about virtually every human. That's why most people won't want to hear this. But once again, it's just a matter of definition. When someone is Christian in the technical sense — and I don't care what religion they fall under — they are acting first from love. In this case, they should still want the luciferic element in them — they want to act with love through the light. Through truth. When they combine these two elements — the love and the light — they are no longer violent or judgmental. In this case, the light is no longer cold. This is why Christ repeatedly told people not to judge, because when they do, they are being luciferic and then the luciferic law applies to them. 'Judge not lest ye be judged,' said Christ. And this is a spiritual fact."

I pursed my lips a moment as I pondered my response. "So in the end, though, you believe the Christ element will reign. That people will act from love, and that they will be free from the control your families currently have over the world?"

"I do," said N.G. "But maybe not in the way most people think of freedom today. These days, people shout for freedom, but they don't want the freedom that Christ offers."

"How do you mean?" I asked. And honestly, this was a more surprising statement to me than his comments about Lucifer.

"Generally when I see people talking about freedom, they mean one of two things. In one case you have folks who say they want people to be free, but they really mean that they want *themselves* to be free because they feel morally adequate for that responsibility. But as soon as someone offends their sense of morality, they feel like *other* people should be controlled by law. They are very right-eous about this and want to apply the light to that person before they apply love. So they are luciferic. And they want to reject the notion that they should love the person rather than judging that person, because they feel *so* justified about their opinion.

Yet loving is exactly what Christ demonstrated. So these people don't actually want the rule of Christ. Not yet. Now this isn't to say that there won't be laws and judgments when Christ reigns, but it will all be experienced so much differently because it will be based in love.

"The other case of people demanding freedom includes those who think that being free means every man for himself. Separate us. Draw lines between us. Draw lines across the land and call them countries. Let us all be independent. Don't tax me, because my money should be mine and shouldn't be used for the collective good. These divisions are extraordinarily luciferic," said N.G. "This doesn't mean that they're *wrong*, so to speak," N.G. assured me, "because they are right and true in a certain light. But only in a cold light. Under the Christ influence, people will see that their independence and interdependence are necessarily intertwined. They're a single reality that people are trying to break in two."

"So you're suggesting that we should be taxed, that my money should go to someone else after I've worked for it? You're saying that's Christian?"

"In a technical sense, yes. Because your wellbeing depends on the wellbeing of all. I also notice that you said 'my money,' assuming that it's yours.

But I assure you that, from the perspective of the prophets, God provides everything, and giving back to the whole is your recognition of this. It also means that you are cared for by others when needed, just as you are caring for them. But keep in mind, I'm describing a time when people cannot bear to think of others suffering and will not only give their money but also their time contributing to the whole. That is the vision we have been given."

"Well," I argued, "this issue of forced taxes, where your money goes to social programs or war or bank bailouts or anything you don't morally believe in, and doing it all under the threat of the IRS, is a major hot button with people across the political spectrum. Not just conspiracy theorists, although a lot of them also believe that the IRS is a fraudulent operation, disallowed by the Constitution."

N.G. laughed, then smiled and looked at me almost fondly. "Well what is fraud?" he asked. "It's Constitutional if the tax amendment was legitimately passed, and that's a matter of perspective. Maybe that's what you call a fraud. Ok. But going back to what gives us the right to control the human population, I told you that — from an Earthly perspective — might makes right. The IRS has the power, so it does what it does. You will, of course, appreciate when I confirm that it is a satanic operation.

But that's because it operates to the benefit of those in power. Put another way, it only takes care of its own. So it is self-preserving, or satanic.

"This is true of much government today — because many politicians look out for their own interests first, and they do so by cozying up to special interests so they can mutually scratch backs, this is all satanic by the definition I've given you. If government were at least luciferic, then it would be consistent, relatively predictable, and relatively just. It would actually look much more the way many people want it to look.

"But again, almost no one today wants the government to be Christian. I don't mean that in terms of the religion, but in terms of love ruling the land. Because right now people want their own interests cared for, or they want to just be left alone. And few understand how well things will function when everyone feels and acts and gives like they're in it together. When you eventually reach a world like that, you won't be paying taxes against your will, and you won't be paying them to programs you believe are immoral. In the true age of Christ, people will give voluntarily and will give abundantly in order to invest in the good of the whole. This is far different from a forced tax system that raises money for, or excludes the taxing of, special interests. The corrupt system you have now is the natural result of a population that votes on single issues and personal benefits.

"When the people themselves only want what is good for the whole rather than what appeals to some personal agenda, the government will begin to reflect that change, and will gradually become more Christian. Ironically, those who want a Christian government are sometimes the most bigoted against those who aren't Christian in name, or who don't live up to their personal ideas of Christianity. But true Christianity is about loving — not intellectually, but from the heart. If they would focus on doing that instead of hating others, the government would actually become Christian in the true sense of the word. That's how you can have an actual Christian government without changing laws or excluding anyone or abridging anyone's rights. Until we reach that age, though, when people overcome separation and act as a true unit, our luciferic families will be in charge."

Chapter 5

At this point, I stood thoughtfully from my chair and began to pace slowly in front of the unlit fireplace. This wasn't a nervous pace, but a reflective one. "So let me get this straight," I said, trying to organize what I'd been told so I could think about what to ask. "You claim that there are three spiritual forces on Earth. The satanic force is the selfish force that thinks first of oneself and what's necessary for survival. This has its use, keeping animals fighting for survival. And since we have animal bodies, we have this element in us. This is what some people call Original Sin."

"Yes," said N.G. nodding.

"But this force isn't the spiritual heritage of humans. We're supposed to express the love and light, or truth, of God. Our satanic bodies, though, couldn't handle God's love without first restricting the satanic element."

"More or less," said N.G. "God's love gives you life. It's in everything. But it couldn't open your hearts without destroying you."

"Ah," said I. The clarification made sense. "So we couldn't embrace the kind of love that we were destined for. First the light had to restrict Satan. And the light is personified by Lucifer, or the Shining One. And since many people have confused Lucifer with Satan, they think of your families as satanic."

"Many people do, yes," said N.G.

"But your families are prophets, sent by God to bring us the light; to restrict Satan; and to do this by controlling the population. Another line of prophets was sent to bring us God's love. But they don't have power until the light has restricted Satan to the point that love can open our hearts without destroying us."

"Yes," said N.G. "We even tried to keep this knowledge in plain sight through a famous allegory shared in the Bible, at a time when symbols were used to express much more than you see in words alone. A similar story is told in different cultures throughout the world."

"What story is that?" I asked, halting my pace and giving him my attention.

"Cain and Abel. You remember the tale?"

"Sure," I said, being well versed in the more popular Biblical stories. "Cain and Abel were brothers, the sons of Adam and Eve. After the Fall, Cain became a farmer and Abel a shepherd. Both made sacrifices to God, with Cain bringing crops and Abel bringing lambs. God accepted Abel's sacrifice but not Cain's, so Cain became jealous and killed his brother."

"Yes," said N.G. "As I said, we once told stories filled with symbolism that gave people much more information than the stories give modern readers. Cain and Abel were the two lines of prophets established to bring humans back to God. From the beginning it was known that Abel's line — the line of Melchizedeks — was the destiny of humankind. The lambs represented God's love, so God accepted that sacrifice. It showed the long-term intent for humanity. That's what was originally meant by the story, see? However, Abel's line couldn't rule humans at that time, as I've explained, because love opening the heart in a satanic being would overwhelm that being. So the Cain prophets had to rule. That's what is represented by him killing Abel.

"Later in the story, God is said to come along looking for Abel, and he asks Cain where his brother is. And Cain basically says, 'I don't know. Am I my brother's keeper?' Which is a luciferic response — an answer that says 'We're all separate, and I'm not responsible for him.' The philosophy of Abel, however, would have been *I AM my brother's keeper*. Big difference.

"So as you can see, Cain's line of prophets — our seven families — were set to rule the masses. Meanwhile, you have all sorts of stories of individual guru and student relationships in many cultures over thousands of years. Those are stories of the Melchizedek line — of the Abel prophets, teaching love to those who had already restricted the satanic element within themselves. They didn't lead the masses, but the rare individual who was ready.

"But in the teachings for the masses through scriptures, you get the teachings of restriction. The light, or the law. Cold hard truths about what you cannot do, or about what you must do with exceptional precision. If you remember the true meaning of Lucifer, then these are luciferic scriptures. Restricting Satan with the light. These laws still apply until love opens the heart and brings someone into a whole new relationship with the law."

I cringed. "You just called people's scriptures luciferic."

"And you keep thinking this is a bad thing," said N.G. in what was almost a scold. "Stop thinking of Lucifer as Satan and you'll be fine. The light is an essential first step on the way to love. I should also point out that this comment applied to scriptures prior to the New Testament. The New Testament brought the first Melchizedek whose mission was to teach the whole world about love. It was the dawn of a new era, when the power would gradually begin shifting from our families to those of the Melchizedek line. These were the first true Christian teachings, as Christ began to reinterpret the old law."

"Are you saying that Jesus was one of those prophets?" I asked, as I took a seat once more and leaned in a bit, growing ever more anxious to get his take on the questions I was asking.

"No," said N.G. "Jesus *was* Melchizedek, namesake of that lineage. He was the Christ, the Path of Return for humanity. He opened up the way for the mass of humans to free the soul and express the divinity within themselves, just as he said they would. So he is not *part* of that family, but actually *authorized* that line of prophets to drive the change that he later came for. Remember, it was always known by the prophets that eventually our family line would give way to the Melchizedek's as God's plan for humanity unfolded. This is why Christ's birth was foretold long before he arrived — because he had already established his lineage on Earth, and it was known that control of the human animal would eventually be enough in place that he could arrive and begin the process of opening the heart with true love, helping the human soul to reach its potential."

If you'd asked me a day before this whether the people behind the New World Order — the same folks who seemed to want to control humanity — would discuss Christ in such a positive light, I probably would have laughed. But at this point, I was so impressed with his thoughts on the topic that I wanted to ask him more. "You said that Christ reinterpreted the old law. How so?"

"Well truth is eternal and unchanging, but it takes different forms to different levels of consciousness. When humans are in a satanic state, they can only relate to the cold, harsh form of light. But that exact same law looks totally different for those who are in a luciferic state — those who have restricted Satan — and are ready to begin opening their hearts. So as I said before, Christ retaught the 'eye for an eye' concept, lifting redemption from a kind of revenge into love by forgiving one's enemies. This is just one example, but I think one of the best I can give."

"So he was speaking to those who were luciferic instead of those who were satanic? People who had embraced the law to the point that they were ready to raise themselves to the next level through love?"

"Yes. Think of it this way: when the satanic element reigns, the body is emphasized or even idolized. This includes lust not only for physical attractiveness and physical relationships, but also a lust for money, food, or anything else that's physical and appeals to the nature of survival and physical pleasure.

"But when the luciferic element reigns, the intellect and personality or ego is emphasized. This is critical for controlling Satan, and *must* be strengthened in order for love to eventually rule. But as it strengthens, then you run into the sins of the mind — pride, envy, idolatry of intelligence and ideas, and so on. This can still involve physical attractions or activities, but for different reasons — ideas of the mind, like dominion and so on. Not for survival reasons, since those would be satanic."

"So Lucifer *is* evil in one sense!" I said.

"Everything is relative," N.G. admitted. "Lucifer is essential to overcoming Satan and is very good in this regard. But he must eventually give way to Christ for these sins to be overcome. When Christ reigns, then the body and ego or personality no longer rule. This is when the true spirit controls the body and mind, and they become willing tools for selfless service.

"And remember what I've said: as long as people remain luciferic, they will be under luciferic law. They will be under the rule of our luciferic families. But the moment they rise up and simply love others, then love will be their law. So when more people focus on expressing the spirit, as Christ taught, our line of prophets will increasingly lose its grip on the world. The New World Order that many people fear will give way to the New World Order that many people hope for — Heaven on Earth, described by the descent of the New Jerusalem in *Revelation*. So the pace of this transition is strictly in the hands of the people themselves."

Chapter 6

As much as I'd fallen under the spell of this unusual story, I was still feeling feisty about the New World Order. I still didn't like the idea of one small group controlling so many other people, and I had some questions that I thought might still trip him up.

"Let's say it's all true," I told N.G. "Let's say there are two lines of prophets sent by God to help humanity. It seems like your control has been overbearing and almost evil. Not the kind of thing that God would order. You claim that your families have set up world leaders and economies from the beginning, yet these leaders and economies have so often been brutal with wars and slavery and poverty all the way along. How do you account for that?"

"First, let's be clear: you are all slaves from the beginning. You're slaves to Satan until you overcome Satan. The satanic element, whether in individuals or in governments, is always brutal, and the luciferic element has done a lot to protect you from that. From the full strength of Satan. Lucifer has also done a great deal to build society and to form justice. Of course as you know, justice without love can also be brutal, especially when satanic and luciferic forces are both involved in the fight for control. So yes, you will celebrate when Christ rescues you from Lucifer by opening the heart of humanity. When you see how peace and health and prosperity can reign, and how your creativity and service can reach their potential, you'll wonder why humanity clung to Lucifer as it has. But Lucifer — the light — has been a literal lifesaver of humanity. Never forget that.

"Second, take a look at the Bible and know that humanity has often been led directly by our line of prophets, rather than by leaders we had to set up. When humans followed the light, things typically went well for them, just as it would if government today became more luciferic and less satanic. This has been true for more than just the Children of Israel. But all too often, the people rejected the prophets and sought kings and emperors instead. This was the satanic influence at work. And because God was leaving people in freedom, he instructed us to give them what they demanded, for the pain of their own choices needed to direct them back toward the light.

"When we had to set up leaders like that, we had to set up leaders that the people would respond to. And this meant setting up those of a satanic mindset — those who were selfish and wanted to protect their own. To some degree, this meant taking care of their people against other nations, because their people were closer to the leader than people of other nations. This also gave the leaders armies, which was about self-preservation as much as it was about preserving their people.

"Yet when they weren't worried about threats from other clans or nations, the leaders were more concerned about their own interests and those of their friends and families than they were about their people. So power always consolidated in the hands of the few to the detriment of the people, and the people were sent to wars to secure ever more wealth and power for the governments. This pattern has repeated because that's what it looks like when governments are run by Satan. In this regard, conspiracy theorists who feel that the government is satanic are right, as I've explained. But they wouldn't even be here to talk about it — certainly not with the freedom they have — if government hadn't been substantially restricted by the light."

"I remember when the Children of Israel rejected the prophets and demanded a king," I said.

"In the Bible, it says they did this because the sons of Samuel were corrupt. They were taking bribes and that sort of thing."

"Yes," said N.G. "Our line of prophets is luciferic and, as we've discussed, there are still sins associated with the light when love is not present. Yet our purpose was only to introduce the light. I cannot apologize for that, since it's what God asked us to do. So while many prophets of the light were indeed close to God, in direct communication with him, and they implemented the law fairly for all people, others took more advantage of their positions of power, as they still do today. But their sins were still those of Lucifer rather than those of Satan. They would have been better for the people than any satanic leader. But yes, as long as humanity is under control of Lucifer, you will have those who apply the light fairly and those who do so with more sinful purposes."

"What about economies?" I asked. "You said you've set those up as well. So you're running the banking systems, including the central banks?"

"To the degree we're able, yes," said N.G.

"When we first spoke on the phone, I said I wanted the people to control the economy and wrest power away from a central banking system. You said that would be ruinous, but I feel like the central banks have driven inflation and devastating economic bubbles. Why do you think it would be worse in the hands of the people?"

"After all I've explained, you should see why. Our families have attempted to run the system from the light, while too many humans would let Satan run the banking system. As it is, we've had to bend to accommodate human greed. People always want more and, in order to satisfy them and prevent uprisings, we have allowed for things like inflation so that people feel they're getting more, that they're somehow doing better than their neighbors or the people of earlier generations even though increased wages are negated by falling value of the money. So yes, it's circular, and it has led to bubbles and short-term pain. The demands of Satan always come back to haunt you. But you have no idea how much worse this would be in the hands of a satanic population. Inflation and bubbles and other problems would have been much worse."

"But with some of the new digital currencies," I argued, "people are purposely trying to eliminate the problems of inflation."

"True, in one sense. As I've said all along, humans are becoming more luciferic and less satanic. So they'll naturally try to lay down laws and systems that treat people as equals. But keep in mind, too, that a digital currency is even less 'real' than printed dollars. Electronic ones and zeroes — a total fantasy. And those who set up these digital economies and start digitally mining the currency first are the ones who will reap massive rewards if the currency gains trust and people use it as a means of exchange. The earliest miners will be those with all the currency to begin the economy, and they will become the new bankers ... just without the ability to print money on a whim in the future. So in that way, it's an advance.

"But never forget," said N.G., "that this possible new economy doesn't eliminate all the satanic desires in people. We were able to keep these in check to some degree with modest inflation. When you cannot do that, Satan will demand an outlet in some other way — if people cannot have more through inflation, then they'll have it by stealing. And as you can already see, criminals are stealing all manner of digital identities and wealth. Until people choose the light, and then later choose love, this problem will only increase and will require ever more control by luciferic forces. Which pretty much brings us full circle, doesn't it?"

I nodded. And by now, understanding the difference between satanic and luciferic elements in people, I saw his point. Yet this made me more hopeful than ever for the eventual reign of love as Christ began to transform the way of humanity.

I pondered a moment more, then addressed the only point that came to mind: "It seems to me like you're not fully in control of things," I said. "Even in your own family, you said some are close to God and some abuse their positions. And then there's the satanic element in the rulers and systems you put in place, and that has to complicate things."

"Exactly right. I said I'd touch on how much we control and how much we don't, and now you're seeing this for yourself. Even within our seven families, we have disputes about how to run economies and countries. So when people imagine that we're behind the scenes with a single plan to control the world, and we pull all the strings directing things toward a single goal, they are mistaken. Yes, we pull a lot of strings, but often toward different goals.

"Besides this, there's the sheer complication of knowing what laws to enact and how to make them work. It's impossible to know how anything will turn out, so there's a lot of trial and error. This is more difficult when the family has different goals. It's even worse when you add the individual ambitions of satanic leaders who bend things for their own benefit.

"Still, the more the leaders become luciferic, the easier it becomes to control things in ways that benefit people more evenly. That's the real goal of the light. Consistent laws that treat everyone the same. Actual justice. But we usually see these progressive shifts in corporations before we do in political and educational systems, because corporations are driven by money, and luciferic businesses yield more money than satanic ones do. And as some businesses are already learning, Christian businesses — in the sense of love driving the business — Christian businesses will be the most lucrative of all."

"And that must be another complication," I noticed. "The influence of Christ with its unique goals."

N.G. breathed deeply, as if his energy were beginning to wane. "Exactly right," he said. "As people gradually open to the Christ force and express their souls, then the Melchizedeks gain power and begin pulling more of the strings. In this case, our power to run things falls away.

"So you see, when people are angry about the idea of a New World Order trying to control them, they should realize all these factors that are interacting. The fact is, they should be glad about the New World Order for the way it has always protected them from Satan; and more than that, they should take responsibility for the energies they allow to play through themselves. If they would seriously restrict Satan in themselves and pray for the love of God to open their hearts, and if they would do this across the globe, the shift would be palpable. We would lose power, the Melchizedeks would rise in power, and before long this globe would look nothing like it does today. It's not my call or yours. It's the call of humanity as a whole."

Though my mind was whirling with the astounding implications of what he'd said, and whirling with the overall details he had shared, N.G. again breathed deeply. He looked content, as if he had done his part. It was clear that, in his mind, the interview was over for now. To my disappointment, he stood up and I followed his example. He was tired, he told me, and felt he had shared what was necessary. With some kindly parting words, then, N.G. led me to the door and shook my hand warmly. "I do hope," he said, "that this puts some things into perspective as you continue with your writing. The conspiracy theories are right about the New World Order in certain ways. But they really haven't touched on its purpose, on its good, or on its goal. They don't understand. What many people fear is more often a function of what they allow by their own actions, by their own inability to restrict the satanic animal inside them. Change is coming indeed," he said. "But let's see just what kind of change the people want.

"And now that you've earned my trust with your earnest questions," he added with a solemn smile, "you get to be our Scribe, if you'll take on the task. Go and share with others what I've shared with you today."

I thanked him, and I was sincere in my thanks, and told him I would do my best to share. Because whether he'd told me the truth of the New World Order or just a well-spun tale, he did give me food for thought. And he opened a world of new questions that I hoped some day I would have the chance to ask. For now, though, I would have to be satisfied with the gems he had given, and with getting those gems written down for others to ponder as well.